W9-AXI-543

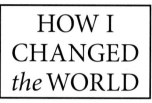

HOW I CHANGED *the* WORLD

Wangari Muta Maathai

WORLD
BOOK

HOW I
CHANGED
the WORLD

Wangari Muta Maathai

WORLD
BOOK

World Book, Inc.
180 North LaSalle Street
Suite 900
Chicago, Illinois 60601
USA

For information about other "How I Changed the World" titles, as well as other World Book print and digital publications, please go to **www.worldbook.com**.

For information about other World Book publications, call 1-800-WORLDBK (967-5325).

For information about sales to schools and libraries, call 1-800-975-3250 (United States) or 1-800-837-5365 (Canada).

Library of Congress Cataloging-in-Publication Data for this volume has been applied for.

How I Changed the World
ISBN: 978-0-7166-2278-9 (set, hc.)

Wangari Muta Maathai
ISBN: 978-0-7166-2283-3 (hc.)

Also available as:
ISBN: 978-0-7166-2289-5 (e-book)

Printed in China by Shenzhen Wing King Tong Paper Products Co., Ltd., Shenzhen, Guangdong
1st printing July 2018

STAFF

Author: Kris Fankhouser

Executive Committee

President
Jim O'Rourke

Vice President and Editor in Chief
Paul A. Kobasa

Vice President, Finance
Donald D. Keller

Vice President, Marketing
Jean Lin

Vice President, International
Maksim Rutenberg

Vice President, Technology
Jason Dole

Director, Human Resources
Bev Ecker

Editorial

Director, New Print
Tom Evans

Managing Editor
Jeff De La Rosa

Editor
Mellonee Carrigan

Librarian
S. Thomas Richardson

Manager, Contracts and Compliance (Rights and Permissions)
Loranne K. Shields

Manager, Indexing Services
David Pofelski

Digital

Director, Digital Product, Development
Erika Meller

Manager, Digital Product
Jon Wills

Manufacturing/ Production

Manufacturing Manager
Anne Fritzinger

Production Specialist
Curley Hunter

Proofreader
Nathalie Strassheim

Graphics and Design

Senior Art Director
Tom Evans

Senior Designer
Don Di Sante

Media Editor
Rosalia Bledsoe

CONTENTS

CHAPTER 1

Growing Up in Kenya

Childhood

Wangari Muta Maathai *(wahn GAHR ee MOO tah mah TY)* (1940-2011) was a Kenyan environmental activist, politician, feminist, and author. She is known primarily as the founder of the Green Belt Movement, a grass-roots organization that worked toward environmental conservation and achieving equal rights for the women of Kenya *(KEHN yuh),* a country on the east coast of the continent of Africa. In 2002, Wangari was elected to Kenya's National Assembly and fought tirelessly to establish free and fair elections in her native country. In 2004, she became the first African woman to be awarded the Nobel Peace Prize.

Wangari Muta was born on April 1, 1940, in the small village of Ihithe *(ih HEE thuh),* Kenya. At the time, Kenya was a colony of the United Kingdom. Ihithe was near the provincial capital of Nyeri *(NYAIR ee)* in the central highlands of Kenya. Wangari's family was Kikuyu *(kih KOO yoo),* the largest of Kenya's 42 ethnic groups, and spoke the Bantu Kikuyu language. The family had lived in the Nyeri district for several generations. Wangari's father, Njugi Muta, was a farmer who raised cattle, goats, and sheep. He was an impressive figure—well over 6 feet (2 meters) tall and muscular. Wangari's mother, Wanjiru Kibicho (who was also known by her Christian name, Lydia) was a loving woman. Thin and shorter than her husband, she looked almost fragile beside him. However, regardless of her stature, she was very strong and a hard worker.

Wangari was her parents' third child and their eldest daughter. Her older brothers were named

Nderitu and Kibicho. Her younger sisters were Murin-gi and Wachatha; they were also known by their respective Christian names, Monica and Beatrice. Wangari was born during the *mbura ya njahi*, Kenya's "season of the long rains." As was the custom, Wangari's mother gave birth to her in the family home. A typical building of the region, it had mud walls, no electricity, and no running water. The delivery was overseen by a midwife, who was assisted by several female family members and friends.

Wangari was aware of her environment from a young age. In her 2006 autobiography, *Unbowed*, she described the land around Ihithe as "lush, green, and fertile." As farmers, her family lived off the land and according to the cycle of Kenya's weather and seasons. Hunger was virtually unknown in the Nyeri district since the soil there was well suited to growing crops of

As was the custom, Wangari was born in the family home, a grass hut similar to the ones shown below, on April 1, 1940. A typical dwelling of the region had mud walls, no electricity, and no running water.

all kinds. Wangari's village also stood in the shadow of Mount Kenya, the second highest peak in Africa at just over 17,000 feet (5,182 meters) above sea level. To the Kikuyu, the mountain was known as *Kirinyaga,* or the "Place of Brightness." When the Kikuyu prayed, celebrated life and death, or performed ritual sacrifices, they did it facing Mount Kenya. It was a sacred place from which all good things flowed: rivers and streams, an abundance of rainfall, and clean drinking water. These beliefs and traditions surrounding Mount Kenya were beginning to fade during Wangari's childhood, but they gave her a deep respect for the world around her.

The European colonization of Africa was another aspect that profoundly affected the Kikuyu—and the entire continent. During the 1800's, European explorers poured into Africa. Accompanying them were Christian missionaries, who came with the express purpose of converting the African population to their religion. The missionaries began their work by visiting villages and attending to the inhabitants' health concerns. After the people were converted to Christianity, the missionaries taught them how to read and write. Before the arrival of the Europeans, the Kikuyu culture functioned through a mostly *oral tradition,* that is, they passed their knowledge from one generation to the next by word of mouth. This was true of most African cultures at the beginning of the 1800's. In time, the coming of the Europeans affected nearly every part of the world in which Wangari was raised.

Once the explorers and missionaries had established a hold on their African territories, the govern-

Wangari's village stood in the shadow of Mount Kenya (shown in the distance). The Kikuyu considered the mountain a sacred place. They did everything facing it. They called it *Kirinyaga,* the "Place of Brightness."

ments in Europe encouraged their people to settle in these new colonies. People from all over Europe—Belgium, France, Great Britain, Germany, Italy, Portugal, and Spain—came and settled throughout Africa. This began in the 1800's and continued well into the 1900's. In 1885, the Berlin Conference formalized what became known as the "Scramble for Africa," a 30-year period in which the major European powers divided almost the entire "Dark Continent" among themselves. ("Dark Continent" is a name that Westerners used for many years to refer to Africa because they knew little about Africa's interior geography, and they mistakenly believed that the people of the interior had not developed any important cultures.) When the

British settlers arrived in Kenya, they found the central highlands to their liking and received title deeds to the land there from the British government in London. British settlers took land the Kikuyu considered their own, and many Kikuyu were forced to work on European farms or to live in poverty. By the 1930's, the British had restricted the native population, including the Kikuyu, to designated plots of land.

By the mid-1900's, nearly 40,000 settlers—most of them from Great Britain—had made their homes in the highlands on about 2,500 farms. The Kikuyu came to refer to that part of their land as the "white

The European colonization of Africa profoundly affected the Kikuyu. After British settlers took their land, many Kikuyu were forced to work on European farms (like the Kikuyu laborers shown here pruning coffee bushes).

highlands." Despite the widespread settlement of the British in Kenya, however, some of the old ways of life remained. The people who inhabited the native reserves could live there as they saw fit. Wangari's father was fortunate enough to own land, which gave Wangari and her family everything they needed for a comparatively stable and prosperous life.

Around the time of Wangari's birth, there were still many Kikuyu who had not converted to Christianity. Three of her grandparents kept to the religious traditions of their birth, but most people of her parents' generation became Christians as adults. Wangari's mother was the holdout in the family and did not convert until she was on her deathbed. Wangari's uncle, Kamunya Muta, was a charismatic leader in the African Independent Church. This progressive church embraced both Roman Catholic and Protestant teachings, while incorporating certain aspects of the Kikuyu culture. Those who converted to Christianity were known as *athomi*, meaning "people who read." The book they read, of course, was the Christian Bible. The *athomi* were given preference by the British colonial administration and were often appointed as chiefs in their communities. Because Wangari's family had converted to Christianity, they enjoyed all the privileges that came with being *athomi*.

Around 1943, a large wave of Kikuyu men left Kenya's native reserves to find jobs on the surrounding white-owned farms. Wangari's father was part of this

Those who converted to Christianity were known as athomi, *meaning "people who read."*

migration. He and about 150,000 young men were among the first generation of Kikuyu to leave their homes and families behind hoping to accumulate wealth in the cash economy of the British colonial administration. When the British began to arrive in Kenya, goats—not money—were the main source of currency among the native population. The life of an average man, for example, was worth about 30 goats, with women and children being worth fewer. However, the British could not accept this system of exchange and brought their own type of economy to Kenya—one that dealt in money. They also wanted to create a labor force but did not want to make the natives work against their will. The British decided to introduce an income tax on Kenyan men that could only be paid in money. Consequently, the Kenyan men had little choice but to move to the cities and towns to look for work.

When the men left their homes to work in Kenya's urban areas, they generally left their wives and children behind. However, this was not the case if they went to work on the farms owned by the European settlers. Njugi found work as a driver and mechanic on the farm of D. N. Neylan and sent word to have his family join him. Neylan, whose farm was near the city of Nakuru in the Rift Valley, gave housing and farming rights to Wangari's father but no title of ownership to the land where he and his family were to live. Nevertheless, Wangari's father soon became one of Neylan's most trusted employees. The next several years in the Rift Valley were a happy time for Wangari and her family.

Early Education

Late in 1947, Wangari's father sent his family back to the Nyeri district and their home village of Ihithe. Sitting his eldest daughter down to explain why, he said, "You are going to Nyeri so you can help your mother take care of your younger sister." However, Wangari's father also had another reason. The time for Wangari to begin school—if she was to do so—was fast approaching. Educating girls was not a common practice among the Kikuyu at the time, but this was not the case in Wangari's family. Unfortunately, there was no school near the farm in the Rift Valley that girls could attend. The European missionaries had established private schools throughout Kenya for the white settlers' children, but the education of Africa's native young people simply was not a priority.

Because Wangari's two older brothers, Nderitu and Kibicho, were enrolled in the primary school in Ihithe, her parents thought it might be the best place for her. Nevertheless, Wangari was anxious about leaving the only home she had ever known and moving back to Ihithe. She was afraid there would be no one of her own age with whom to play, but her father did his best to reassure her. "Don't worry," he told her. "There are still many children in my homestead." Wangari was also sad about leaving her youngest sister behind. Muringi, eager to help her parents with the farm chores, had badly injured her leg and remained with her father in Nakuru until she recovered.

After a long bus ride through the wilds of Kenya, Wangari, her mother, and her sister Wachatha arrived in the village of Ihithe. Friends and relatives gathered to welcome them home. Among them were Wangari's cousins, the children of her uncle Kamunya. Wangari, her mother, and her sister lived with Kamunya's family while a house was built for them on the homestead. Before long, Wangari became friends with her cousins and quickly felt at home in Ihithe. Still, it was a very different place compared to the farm in the Rift Valley. Nakuru, meaning "dusty place" in Maasai (*mah SY*), a native language of the area, stood in sharp contrast to the green, fertile land surrounding Ihithe. Once their house was finished, Wangari's mother gave her a small garden—about 15 square feet—on the family's farm. She instructed Wangari how to plant and care for crops, telling her that the small plot of land would be her responsibility. Tending to her new garden soon became Wangari's favorite thing to do. She spent hours and hours planting and raising her sweet potatoes, beans, and maize (corn).

Tending to her new garden soon became Wangari's favorite thing to do.

Once the family was settled in its new home, Wangari's brother Nderitu asked his mother a pointed question. "How come Wangari doesn't go to school like the rest of us?" he demanded to know. "There's no reason why not," his mother answered. With no formal education herself, Wangari's mother had never learned to read or write. However, she was determined to give her daughter greater opportunities in life. She went to Kamunya to seek his consent as the head of their homestead. Kamunya, who had recently put one of his own daughters in school, wholeheartedly agreed

Wangari attended the local primary school in her village at a time when it was uncommon for girls to be educated. The school was typical for its time, with mud walls, an earthern floor, and a tin roof (like the one shown at left).

with the idea. Shortly afterward, Wangari joined her brothers and cousins in school.

Presbyterian missionaries had founded Ihithe Primary School. Some of its teachers were native to Ihithe, but many came from far away. All the teachers, however, lived together in a large house on the school compound. The school itself was typical for its time, with mud walls, an earthen floor, and a tin roof. The student body consisted of young children as well as several adults who were just entering the education system. At Ihithe Primary School, Wangari learned to read and write. Over the next several years, she took classes in mathematics, geography, and English, among others. Outside of school, Wangari remained attentive to the natural world around her. Ihithe was near Aberdare National Park. She often explored its paths, hoping to get a glimpse of the elephants, monkeys, and leopards that made their home there.

Though Wangari never encountered these wild animals, her mother told her not to be afraid of them.

In 1951, when Wangari was 11 years old, she was sent to St. Cecilia's Intermediate Primary School in Nyeri. St. Cecilia's was a boarding school at the Mathari Catholic Mission that was run by the Consolata Missionary Sisters from Italy. Going to St. Cecilia's made Wangari both happy and sad. She was glad to be sent there with one of her cousins, also named Wangari, but the idea of being separated from her mother for the first time in her life frightened her. However, St. Cecilia's had a reputation for quality education and strict discipline. Wangari's family had only one concern in sending her away—they were afraid she might convert to Catholicism and become a nun. Kikuyu women were expected to marry and have children. If Wangari became a nun, it would be a major loss to her community.

Outside of school, Wangari remained attentive to the natural world around her.

After Wangari arrived at St. Cecilia's, she became homesick. One of the nuns at the boarding school sensed this and did everything she could to help Wangari adjust. Her name was Sister Germana, and she quickly became a mother figure to Wangari. Another nun, named Sister Christiana, who had come to Kenya from South Africa, acted as Wangari's chief disciplinarian. Over the next four years, these two women—along with the other nuns at St. Cecilia's—had a profound impact on Wangari. After many lessons about Christianity, she decided to convert to Catholicism and took the baptismal name Mary Josephine. In time, most of Wangari's family came to accept her decision and supported her.

In 1952, toward the end of Wangari's first year at St. Cecilia's, the Mau Mau rebellion erupted in Kenya. The military uprising was aimed at ending British rule. It was politically dominated by members of the Kikuyu community. Wangari was protected from the conflict at St. Cecilia's, but there were few Kikuyu families whose lives were unaffected. Wangari's own mother was attacked by a group of men thought at the time to be Mau Mau rebels, though she was not seriously injured. The fighting also created a widespread sense of panic and terror in Kenya's white community. This led the British governor, Sir Evelyn Baring, to declare a state of emergency. The Mau Mau rebellion lasted until Oct. 21, 1956, when the British captured and later executed the rebel leader, Dedan Kimathi.

The Mau Mau rebellion erupted in Kenya in 1952, near the end of Wangari's first year at St. Cecilia's Intermediate Primary School. In this image, British colonial authorities round up locals in search of Mau Mau rebels in Kenya.

That same year, Wangari graduated from St. Cecilia's at the head of her class.

Because of her outstanding academic performance at St. Cecilia's, Wangari was admitted to the prestigious Loreto High School. Loreto was in the small town of Limuru just outside the capital of Nairobi. It was Kenya's only Catholic high school for African girls and attracted students from all over the country. While at Loreto, Wangari attended Mass every Sunday. She also developed a mature worldview and a deep sense of justice. "After my education by the nuns," she wrote years later, "I emerged as a person who believed that society is inherently good and that people generally act for the best. … A positive attitude toward life and fellow human beings is healthy—not only for one's peace of mind but also to bring about change." When she graduated from Loreto in 1959, Wangari hoped to attend Makerere University in Kampala, Uganda. Known as the "Oxford of East Africa," Makerere University was an ambitious goal for Wangari, even with her excellent academic performance. (The University of Oxford, located in Oxford, England, is one of the world's most famous institutions of higher learning.) In the end, attending Makerere was a goal that went unfulfilled for Wangari due to an unexpected opportunity that took her much farther from home.

Studies Abroad

By the time Wangari graduated from high school, the era of colonialism in most of Africa was coming to an end. Kenya remained a colony of the United Kingdom until 1963, but many knew that independence was not far off. In 1957, black Kenyans were given the right to vote in elections for the first time. Two years later, the British government invited several Kenyan politicians to London for discussions about the new political order. These leaders understood that Kenya would need well-educated men and women to fill key positions in the new government once the British departed. Among these farsighted politicians was Tom Mboya, one of the founding fathers of the Republic of Kenya.

In the late 1950's, Mboya approached Senator John F. Kennedy, who later became president of the United States, and Martin Luther King, Jr., a leader in the American civil rights movement, to help create education opportunities for African students. Mboya wanted to provide scholarships to schools in

She was among the 300 Kenyan students chosen to begin their studies in the United States in September 1960.

Western nations for the best and brightest young people in Kenya and other African countries that were moving toward independence. Senator Kennedy agreed to fund the program and pay for the students' transportation expenses through the Joseph P. Kennedy Foundation. Eventually known as the Kennedy Airlift, this effort brought nearly 600 young Kenyans to study at various colleges and universities across the United States.

When the Roman Catholic bishop in Nairobi heard about the Kennedy Airlift, he wanted the students in his schools to take part in it. As it happened, Wangari was in the right place at the right time. She was among the 300 Kenyan students chosen to begin their studies in the United States in September 1960. Wangari was extremely excited about the opportunity. She later said that arriving in New York City that summer was "like landing on the moon." Fortunately, Wangari was with her friend Agatha Wangeci, with whom she had studied at St. Cecilia's, and they met many other young African students who had just arrived. At their orientation, they were given a tour of the United Nations, where dignitaries from around the world welcomed them to America.

Wangari and Agatha did not stay long in New York. After their orientation, the two young women boarded a Greyhound bus and began their long journey to the Midwest. Their destination was Mount St. Scholastica College (known today as Benedictine College) in Atchison, Kansas. Run by nuns of the Order of St. Benedict, the school was founded in 1863 and commonly referred to as "the Mount" by its students, who proudly called themselves "Mounties."

When they arrived at the Mount, Wangari and Agatha received a warm reception from the nuns and other students. "They were very welcoming," Wangari later said, "exhibiting the overflowing enthusiasm typical of Americans." This friendly atmosphere stood in stark contrast to the treatment she and Agatha had received in Indiana. Stopping at a café there during their bus ride to Kansas, they had been refused service because of the color of their skin. This encounter with discrimination in the United States came as a shocking surprise to Wangari, and she quickly realized that American society was more complex than she had originally thought.

Focusing on her studies, Wangari found that the Mount was quite different from the Catholic schools she had attended in Kenya. The education she received at the Mount was broad-based, demanding, and quite progressive. In February 1961, she wrote a letter to her brother Nderitu, saying, "This semester I am taking zoology, psychology, scripture, English composition, modern European history, and sports. It's quite a bit of work, enough to keep my little brain busy." The landscape of Kansas was also very different from that of Kenya. Whereas her homeland was full of hills and mountains with breathtaking vistas, Wangari described Kansas as being "flat as a pancake." However, she enjoyed taking long walks along the banks of the Missouri River in her free time. Wangari also experienced snowfall for the first time in her life. The only snow she had seen before was in the distance atop Mount Kenya.

Wangari (shown here as a young woman) was among 300 Kenyan students chosen to study abroad in the United States in 1960. She graduated in 1964 from Mount St. Scholastica College (now Benedictine College) in Atchison, Kansas.

Wangari's years at the Mount were happy ones, and she made several lifelong friends during that time. She was impressed by the warmth and generosity that some of her classmates showed her during the holiday seasons. One of her friends, Florence Conrad, was especially kind. Because Wangari was unable to return to Kenya for just a short stay, Florence and her family invited her to spend the holidays with them. Wangari usually spent Easter, Thanksgiving, and

Christmas at the Conrad home in nearby Wichita, Kansas. This was particularly meaningful in the 1960's, when there was so much conflict and racial tension in the United States. At the time, much of the country was still *segregated*, that is, blacks were separated from whites in public places and treated as second-class citizens. Fortunately, other than the incident at the café in Indiana, Wangari did not experience any explicit discrimination during her time in America.

During her last year at the Mount, Wangari received some wonderful news from Kenya. On Dec. 12, 1963, her beloved homeland had at last gained its independence from the United Kingdom. Elections for representatives of the new government had been held the previous May. Jomo Kenyatta took office as the country's first prime minister. The following year, he became the first president of the Republic of Kenya. The news came as a welcome relief to Wangari. Only a few weeks earlier, U.S. President John F. Kennedy, the man who had helped make her education in the United States possible, had been assassinated by Lee Harvey Oswald, in Dallas, Texas. When Kennedy died on Nov. 22, 1963, a deep sense of sadness

Kenyan President Jomo Kenyatta (left) talks with Kenyan politician Tom Mboya during a celebration of Kenya's independence in 1963. Mboya had been considered by many to be Kenyatta's successor before he was assassinated on July 5, 1969.

took hold of the country. The announcement of Kenya's independence allowed Wangari to experience feelings of happiness and joy for the first time since Kennedy's death. She and some of her friends from the Mount celebrated her country's newfound freedom with the small Kenyan community in Lawrence, Kansas. There, they sang and danced until the early hours of the morning.

In the spring of 1964, Wangari graduated from Mount St. Scholastica College with a Bachelor of Science degree in biology, with minors in chemistry and German. She immediately applied to the University of Pittsburgh in Pennsylvania and was accepted. Through the Africa-American Institute, she received a scholarship and began her studies to obtain a master's degree in biological sciences. Pittsburgh was a much larger city that Atchison. Like many manufacturing cities in the United States in the 1960's, Pittsburgh was just coming to terms with the long-term effects of the pollution that had begun 100 years earlier when the area became heavily industrialized. The city had recently started a program to clean up its air. This was Wangari's first experience with environmental restoration, and it made a deep impression on her.

In 1965, as Wangari was finishing her studies in Pittsburgh, she was interviewed by a group of people from the University College of Nairobi (later renamed the University of Nairobi), including the vice-chancellor. Through the government of the newly independent Republic of Kenya, they knew she was about to graduate and offered her a job as a research assistant to one of the professors of zoology. Shortly after the interview, Wangari received a letter confirming her new position with the university. She was told to report on Jan. 10, 1966. Taking the job meant that Wangari would miss her own graduation, but she knew it was an opportunity that she could not turn down. After more than five years in the United States, she was filled with conflicting emotions. Wangari was sad to leave her friends in America behind, but she was also excited to be going back home.

Family Life

Upon returning to Kenya in January 1966, Wangari decided to start using the name her parents had given her at birth. She was given the name Miriam when she was first baptized as a Christian. Throughout her childhood, she was known as Miriam Wangari, and her father's surname, Muta, was set aside. After becoming a Catholic, she dropped the name Miriam and was called Mary Josephine (or Mary Jo) Wangari by her family. This was how she was known at the time she left for the United States. After returning to Kenya, she embraced her father's surname once again and proudly called herself Wangari Muta.

Wangari made her way to the University College of Nairobi four days after her arrival at Nairobi International Airport and a brief visit with her family. She proudly reported for her first day of work as a research assistant in the department of zoology. When Wangari met with the person she expected to be her supervisor, he told her that the job had been given to someone else. "But you wrote me this letter!" Wangari protested, holding it up for the man to see. "I've come all the way from the United States of America!" She was devastated by this news and did not know what to do. After her time in America, Wangari had begun to think that there would be no limit to her new life and career in Africa. She soon discovered that tribalism, sexism, and other forms of discrimination and corruption in Kenyan society would be the greatest barriers to her unfulfilled dreams.

While looking for a new job, Wangari lived in Nairobi with her brother Nderitu and his wife, Elizabeth. Nderitu had recently been named assistant dean of the School of Veterinary Medicine at the University College of Nairobi—the same institution that had cheated Wangari out of the job in its department of zoology. Through her brother, Wangari met Professor Reinhold Hofmann. Hofmann was looking for a research assistant, and Wangari wasted no time in applying for the job. During the interview, Hofmann was pleased to learn that Wangari's background in biology made her the ideal candidate. Wangari was thrilled when he offered her the position. Over the next several years, she worked hard, registered for her doctorate, and eventually became part of the research and teaching team of the university's department of veterinary anatomy.

In April 1966, shortly after starting her new job, Wangari met Mwangi Mathai, the man who would become her husband. Mwangi had grown up in Njoro, a small town in the Rift Valley not far from Nakuru. Like Wangari, he had also studied in the United States. After working for various corporations in Kenya, he had entered politics. Before long, Wangari's relationship with Mwangi became serious, and they talked about marriage. Wangari wanted to have a family. However, she did not want to sacrifice her education and career, and so the two of them decided to wait. In 1967, Professor Hofmann spoke to Wangari about the possibility of doing research for her doctorate in veterinary anatomy at the University of Giessen in Germany. Wangari was excited by the opportunity and left later that year for Germany. During her time in Germany, Mwangi wrote her many letters urging her to come back to Kenya as soon as possible so they could start their family.

In the spring of 1969, Wangari returned to Kenya and the University College of Nairobi. She rejoined the faculty as an assistant lecturer in veterinary anatomy and continued to do research for her doctorate. In May, Wangari and Mwangi were married. She was 29 and he was 34. They decided to have two ceremonies. The first was a traditional Kikuyu wedding held on the Muta farm in Nakuru. The second was a Catholic service at Our Lady Queen of Peace Church in Nairobi, where Wangari wore a floor-length, white Western-style dress and a veil and carried a bouquet of flowers. Within the year, the couple had their first child, a boy named Waweru. Two more children soon followed. Their daughter Wanjira, named in honor of Mwangi's mother, was born in 1971, and their second son, Muta, named after Wangari's father, was born in 1974. It was a happy time for Wangari and her family. She enjoyed being a mother and looked forward to what the future would bring.

CHAPTER 2

"Liberated from Fear and from Silence"

The Call to Social Action

The year 1969 was an important one for Wangari and her family, and it presented several challenges for them. That year, her second-oldest brother, Kibicho, died of pancreatitis at the age of 39. (Pancreatitis is a disease that involves inflammation of the pancreas and causes severe pain in the abdomen.) Though her brother Nderitu had been more influential in Wangari's life, she was closer to Kibicho. His death deeply saddened Wangari, but her husband could offer only little support because of his busy schedule. Mwangi had decided to run for a seat in Kenya's Parliament, and this kept him away from home more than he or Wangari wanted. One day, Mwangi surprised his wife by coming home early, but Wangari instantly knew something was wrong by the terrible look on his face. "What's happened?" she asked worriedly. "Mboya has been killed," Mwangi answered. Wangari was shocked to learn that Tom Mboya, who had been instrumental in the Kennedy Airlift, had been assassinated. Without him, she would have never been able to study in America.

Mboya had been considered by many to be the obvious successor to President Kenyatta. His death created a lot of mistrust and confusion among Kenya's different ethnic groups. When national elections took place in December 1969, Mwangi narrowly lost his bid to become a member of Parliament. Shortly afterward, President Kenyatta, head of the Kenyan African National Union (KANU), banned KANU's chief rival, the Kenya People's Union. This effectively put an end to Kenya's multiparty system for the next 23 years.

Mwangi was disappointed by his loss at the polls, and the political atmosphere of Kenya remained tense. Nevertheless, life went on for Wangari and her husband. In 1971, she completed her research in the field of veterinary anatomy and became the first woman in East Africa to receive a doctoral degree. At her graduation, Wangari received her diploma from President Kenyatta himself, who, as head of state, also served as chancellor of the University of Nairobi (which had been renamed in 1970). It was a great achievement for Wangari, and she was filled with pride.

After receiving her doctorate, Wangari continued to teach at the University of Nairobi, and she enjoyed a successful career there. In 1974, she became a senior lecturer in anatomy. Two years later, she was named the chairperson of the department of veterinary anatomy. Finally, in 1977, she became an associate professor. While Wangari was the first woman to hold any of these positions, she continued to face discrimination in the workplace. The university's full benefits were not available to female employees, and women were generally paid less than their male counterparts. Determined to fight this injustice, Wangari and one of her female colleagues, Vertistine ("Vert") Mbaya, went to the university's administration and demanded an

In 1971, Wangari became the first woman in East Africa to receive a doctoral degree. It was presented to her by Kenyan President Jomo Kenyatta himself (below), who also served as chancellor of the University of Nairobi.

explanation. When they did not receive a satisfactory answer, they turned to the Academic Staff Association. However, because the association did not have the legal status to negotiate for benefits, Wangari and Vert attempted to form a union to take the matter to Kenya's courts. This strategy failed, but the university later met many of Wangari and Vert's demands.

From this struggle, Wangari learned the importance of remaining true to one's own principles. She also realized that her campaign for equality could not be limited to her university. There were broader concerns to consider. During the 1970's, she became active in several civic organizations in Nairobi. Among them were the local branch of the Kenya Red Cross, of which she became the director in 1973, and the Kenya Association of University Women. Both organizations had been founded by the British when Kenya was still a colony. Originally, they were staffed almost entirely by the wives of colonial officials, but Africans gradually replaced the women after independence. In 1974, Wangari also joined the Environment Liaison Centre. It was founded earlier that same year to ensure the participation of nongovernmental organizations in the work of the United Nations Environment Programme (UNEP). Headquartered in Nairobi, UNEP was established after the United Nations Conference on the Human Environment, which had been held in Stockholm, Sweden, in 1972. UNEP was the first and only agency of the United Nations devoted to international envi-

> *. . . for real change to take place, they would have to go beyond their own borders . . .*

ronmental causes. It was also the only one based in the developing world.

Around this time, Wangari had joined the National Council of Women of Kenya (NCWK). Founded in 1964, the NCWK was an organization whose purpose was to unify women's groups throughout Kenya. The leadership of the NCWK was made up of women who were successful in their chosen careers and able to provide moral support for one another. Though most of its leaders came from Kenya's upper class, they focused on the needs of poor and deprived women living in the rural parts of the country. Some of the most serious issues that these women faced included lack of access to clean water and insufficient food to eat and firewood to burn for fuel. Through her work with the NCWK and other organizations, Wangari gradually became aware of the dangers posed to Kenya's natural environment and the many other problems associated with this nationwide threat.

Planting Trees in Kenya

In the mid-1970's, women in countries around the world began to recognize that changes needed to be made in society. Many understood that, for real change to take place, they would have to go beyond their own borders and bring the world's attention to the local and regional challenges they faced. Fortunately, many political leaders were giving them the space to do just that. In June 1975, coinciding with the observance of the International Women's Year, 4,000 women from around the world—representing 133 nations—assembled in Mexico City for the first United

Wangari believed that planting trees would help solve some of Kenya's problems caused by a deteriorating environment. This image shows a barren landscape in Kenya, where the lack of food and water are some of the problems faced by the country's people.

Nations conference on women's issues. Wangari did not attend this gathering because of duties to work and family, but several members of the NCWK made the journey to Mexico City. When they returned to Kenya, they reported to the NCWK what had been discussed at the conference. The topics included water, energy, nutrition, and a long list of other important issues. As Wangari listened to their report, she realized that many of the countries represented at the conference shared the same concerns faced by the people of Kenya. Their message was clear. Something had to be done about the lack of clean water and reliable and renewable energy sources.

At the same time, the women who attended the conference in Mexico City had concluded that the world needed to address the challenges faced by rural women. These women lived in poverty, they lacked the proper resources, and their social and economic situations would fail to sustain them over the long term. For Wangari, everything suddenly became clear. All these issues were related and interconnected. They were problems clearly created by a deteriorating environment. The lack of food and water was just a symptom of the underlying causes of environmental degradation. Deforestation (cutting down trees on a large scale), poor farming practices, and the resulting soil loss were at the heart of the problems faced by the people of Kenya. In time, these things would come to affect everyone in the country, not just poverty-stricken women living in rural areas.

> *Wangari came up with the simple, yet inspired, idea of planting trees in Kenya.*

Wangari realized something had to be done. "I have always been interested in finding solutions," she later said. "This is, I believe, a result of my education as well as my time in America—to think of what can be done rather than worrying about what cannot." To this end, Wangari came up with the simple, yet inspired, idea of planting trees in Kenya. If enough trees were planted throughout the country, they would provide the wood that Kenyan women needed to build fires and cook nutritious meals for their families. When fully grown, these trees would offer shade for Kenya's people and their animals. Trees would also help bind the soil and, in the case of fruit trees, provide food. Also, trees would provide a place for birds and other small animals to build nests, thus bringing greater vitality to the land and helping to restore ecosystems.

By the end of 1974, Wangari came up with an idea about how to launch her campaign of planting trees throughout Kenya. That same year, Mwangi reentered politics. He was determined to try again, despite having run for a seat in Kenya's Parliament in 1969 and losing the election. Wangari wholeheartedly supported her husband's decision and worked hard to make sure he won the second time around. With her full-time job at the university and three children to raise, she knew this would be difficult. However, Wangari and Mwangi were equally committed to making a difference in the lives of their fellow Kenyans. By this time, unemployment had become a major issue in the country. During his campaign,

Wangari plants a tree at a 1977 UN conference in Nairobi, Kenya, with environmentalist Richard St. Barbe Baker (right, in white suit) and Kenyan Chief Josiah Njonjo (far left), the co-founders of the conservation organization Men of the Trees (now known as the International Tree Foundation).

Mwangi promised he would create more jobs if people voted for him. In the end, Mwangi won his election. As a member of Parliament, he represented the people living in Lang'ata, a suburb of Nairobi.

Wangari was happy for him and proud of his achievement, but she remained concerned about all the promises he had to make to get elected. "What are you going to do with all the people you promised the jobs to?" she asked Mwangi. "Don't worry," he replied. "They won't remember." However, Wangari knew that Mwangi was wrong. People would remember his campaign promises and expect him to deliver on them. It was then that Wangari came up with the idea of creating her own business that would combine her ideas about the environment with her husband's political career. Called Envirocare Ltd., this company had two main objectives. The first was to put as many unemployed people to work as possible, thus helping to keep Mwangi's campaign promises. The second was to have Envirocare's employees plant trees for conservation wherever they could.

The district that Mwangi represented in Parliament contained both rich and poor alike, including a large part of the Kibera slum. Many of the wealthy citizens of Lang'ata lived on vast estates with lush gardens. The owners of these estates needed workers to look after their gardens. It was Wangari's hope to give jobs to unemployed men and women from the poor parts of Lang'ata. This, in turn, would fulfill the labor needs of the city's wealthy landowners. Envirocare would also plant trees in areas around Lang'ata that had none. In the process, the company would help to beautify Nairobi and its surroundings. Wangari thought this was the perfect solution. She was confident the wealthy residents of Lang'ata would support her idea and that everyone would benefit.

During Mwangi's campaign, Wangari had met a man named Kimathi wa Murage, a government official in charge of Karura Forest to the north of Nairobi. When she told him about her hopes to establish a tree nursery and provide jobs for the unemployed of Lang'ata, Murage was impressed with her ideas. Shortly afterward, he gave her permission to start a tree nursery next to the government land that he oversaw. Excited by Murage's offer, Wangari immediately hired a young man named Charles Githogori to look after it. Wangari's first tree nursery filled her with great hope for the future.

However, Envirocare soon ran into problems. Many of Lang'ata's wealthy citizens did not like the idea of poor people wandering about the gardens on their large estates and refused to hire them. Funding also became a problem. Many of the landowners refused to pay Envirocare in advance. This meant that Wangari, who was not a wealthy woman, had to pay the upfront costs out of her own pocket. Before long, Envirocare was forced to go out of business. While Wangari was discouraged by this failure, other opportunities quickly presented themselves. Through a mutual friend, she met Maurice String, the executive director of UNEP. When Wangari told String about her efforts with Envirocare, he thought that planting trees in Kenya was a wonderful idea. "That's what *we're* trying to encourage at UNEP," he said.

In June 1976, after several conversations with String, Wangari was invited to attend the first United Nations conference on human settlements. Known as Habitat I, the conference took place in Vancouver, British Columbia, Canada. Habitat I examined the rapid growth of cities around the world and some of the resulting problems, such as air pollution. Margaret Mead, a noted American anthropologist, and Barbara Ward, a British economist and journalist, were among the speakers at the conference. It was the first time Wangari had attended a global meeting of this kind, and it made a deep impression on her. Upon returning to Kenya, she was reenergized and determined to make her ideas work.

The following year, the NCWK invited Wangari to talk about her experience at the Habitat I conference. Shortly afterward, she became a member of its executive committee. Wangari proposed that the NCWK begin planting throughout Kenya to assist its rural members and help meet their needs. The executive committee agreed and encouraged her to put this idea into action. Wangari thought it would be wise to place her tree planting campaign within President Kenyatta's idea of community mobilization, which was known by the national slogan *Harambee!* (meaning "Let's all pull together!" in Kiswahili, the language of Africa's Swahili people). She called her project "Save the Land Harambee."

On June 5, 1977, Kenya celebrated World Environment Day with a grand parade. It began at the Kenyatta International Conference Centre in downtown Nairobi and ended in Kamukunji Park on the outskirts of the city. There, the highlight of the event was a tree-planting ceremony sponsored by the NCWK. Seven trees were planted to honor past leaders of Kenya's different ethnic groups. Among the types of trees planted that day were a Nandi flame, a broad-leaved cordia, an African fig tree, and an East African yellow wood. These seven trees formed the first of the so-called "green belts" that would adorn the barren land of Kenya. This was the birth of what became known as the Green Belt Movement. By the end of the year, news of the NCWK's tree-planting project had begun to spread. Within months, schools, churches, and farms all over the country were eager to set up their own programs.

"The future of the planet concerns all of us, and all of us should do what we can to protect it."

This success made the NCWK consider its tree-planting project on a larger scale. In time, they came up with the idea to plant a tree for every person in Kenya—15 million in total. This was reflected by their new slogan: "One person, one tree."

Wangari was extremely pleased by these develop-ments. After so many disappointments, her ideas were finally taking off. Leading the way, she was often down in the soil on her hands and knees, planting trees, working side by side with women in rural areas. Wangari was a highly educated woman, but she found this work to be completely natural. However, many of Kenya's politicians ridiculed her for doing manual labor alongside the country's poor. Her answer to them was simple yet powerful: "Education, if it means anything at all, should not take people away from the land, because educated people are in a better position to understand what is being lost. The future of the planet concerns all of us, and all of us should do what we can to protect it."

Divorce

When the summer of 1977 began, Wangari's life was happy, and she enjoyed many satisfactions. She had a good job at the University of Nairobi, she had a successful husband and three beautiful children, and her program of planting trees across Kenya was now in full swing. Then one day in July Wangari came home from work and was shocked by what she saw. Some of the paintings that had hung on the walls were missing and packing material lay on the floor. As she walked through the house, Wangari noticed that the television, the record player, and other furnishings were gone as well. "What happened?" she asked the woman who took care of the children and helped with the housework. "Papa Mathai packed all his things in his car and left," the woman answered. Wangari was stunned. In an instant, the last eight years she had spent with Mwangi ran through her mind—their courtship and wedding, the birth of their children, all the joy and sadness they had shared together. She realized that part of her life was now over.

The days that followed Mwangi's departure were sad and lonely for Wangari. She struggled to understand why her marriage had fallen apart. In time, it became clear. Both Wangari and Mwangi had demanding jobs, along with the responsibility of raising three children. Because both had been educated in the

United States, they were under a lot of pressure to do well. Kenyan society was very much a "man's world" when Wangari and Mwangi were growing up. Boys were provided education before girls, and men were expected to achieve more than women. In the Mathai home, it became an "unspoken problem" when Wangari received her doctorate. Mwangi became envious of his wife's accomplishment, though Wangari did not realize this at the time.

Wangari came to realize that the attitudes in Kenyan society about husbands and wives were a large part of the problem. Quite naturally, it formed Mwangi's view of their relationship. "He saw me through the mirror given to him by society," Wangari later wrote, "rather than through his own eyes. He was a product of his times and felt toward educated women the way most men in Kenya did then." This placed pressure on men to behave in certain ways. Even if wives were more educated or more successful, their husbands were expected to remain in control of their households. Society dictated that men had to prove they were the ones in charge. Unfortunately, Wangari did not realize until it was too late that her success was becoming a source of friction in her marriage. For some time, Wangari hoped that reconciliation with her husband would be possible, but Mwangi did not feel the same way.

In 1979, the couple went to court. After two years of separation, Mwangi was ready to formally and legally end their marriage. The laws governing divorce in force in Kenya at that time had been established when the country was still a colony of the United

Kingdom. Divorces were granted only for such very serious reasons as adultery, insanity, or extreme cruelty. This system made some people who sought to end their marriage tell lies about their spouses and bring wild accusations against them. Unfortunately, this was the course of action that Mwangi took. He told the court that Wangari was a cruel wife, that she had committed adultery, and that she was responsible for his high blood pressure. These charges stunned Wangari. She could not believe that Mwangi would make up such terrible things about her. Originally, she hoped to keep their divorce proceedings a private affair. Because Wangari denied the charges, however, a trial became mandatory.

Wangari was not ready for the trial when it began. It was difficult on her and the children. The trial lasted about three weeks, but to Wangari it seemed to drag on for years. Much of her private life became part

Although Wangari was a highly educated woman, she was often down in the soil on her hands and knees, planting trees, working side by side with women in rural areas. Many politicians ridiculed her for doing manual labor alongside Kenya's poor.

of the official court record. Because Mwangi was a member of Parliament, reporters covered the court proceedings as if they were a soap opera. During the trial, Mwangi said that Wangari was "too educated, too strong, too successful, too stubborn, and too hard to control." When this was reported in the newspapers, Wangari received little sympathy from the press. Like many people in Kenya at the time, most reporters and editors assumed that if a marriage fell apart, it was the wife's fault for not obeying her husband.

Wangari did not intend to go down without a fight, but she knew she was facing an uphill battle. Unfortunately, some of the evidence that Wangari had to disprove her husband's lies about having high blood pressure was stolen from her car during the trial. In the end, the judge ruled in favor of Mwangi. When their divorce was finalized, Wangari was devastated. "I felt cheated, betrayed, taken advantage of, and misused," she wrote years later. "I walked away in pain. I was in pieces, and worse was yet to come."

Adding insult to injury, Mwangi told Wangari that he did not want her to continue to use his surname. For Wangari, this was a step too far. She had not wanted to use his name in the first place. She also did not like being treated like an object whose name could be changed by a new owner. To deal with her overwhelming feelings of rejection, Wangari kept her husband's surname in defiance of his wishes. However, she decided to add another "a" to Mathai. This reminded Wangari that she would always share a connection with Mwangi, yet at the same time she had a new identity: Wangari Muta Maathai.

Difficult Times

About a week after the trial ended, Wangari was contacted by Salim Lone, a Kenyan journalist and editor of *Viva* magazine. As an advocate of free expression, he was interested in her case and wanted to do an interview. When Lone asked Wangari what she thought about the judge's ruling in her divorce case, she did not hold back. She claimed there had not been enough evidence to dissolve her marriage with Mwangi in the eyes of the law. That meant, she said, that the judge was either incompetent or corrupt. When the judge learned what Wangari had said, he threatened her with contempt of court. Nevertheless, Wangari refused to take her statement back. She did not believe she had done anything wrong.

This led the government to bring charges against both Wangari and Lone. Lone was given the choice of paying a fine of 40,000 Kenyan shillings (about 396 U.S. dollars)—a large amount of money—or spending six months in jail. However, Wangari was given no such choice. She was found guilty of contempt and sentenced to six months in prison. She was immediately arrested and sent to Lang'ata Women's Prison in Nairobi. She was not even given the chance to return home to explain the situation to her children and say goodbye to them. Fortunately, she was released after only three days when her lawyer drew up a statement that served as a formal apology to the court.

Following her release from prison, money remained an issue for Wangari. Kenyan law did not require Mwangi to assist her in any way after the divorce. Wangari was in debt, had little savings, and the money she owed in legal fees was substantial. She still had her job at the university, but her salary was not enough to support her and three children. Fortunately, an opportunity for extra income arose through her friend Vert Mbaya. The United Nations Development Programme was looking for someone to take a six-month assignment with the Economic Commission for Africa that involved investigating the livestock industry in Zambia. Once Wangari convinced Mwangi to watch over the children for the duration of the assignment, she happily took the job.

In 1979, Wangari decided to run for the post of NCWK chairperson. However, Kenya's new president, Daniel arap Moi, opposed her candidacy. He believed that Kikuyu already had too much power in the country and wanted to limit their influence. Wangari lost the election by only three votes. However, she was overwhelmingly chosen to be the vice-chair of the NCWK. The following year, she ran for chairperson again. This time, though she was still opposed by the Kenyan government, Wangari won. Nevertheless, President Moi's regime (system of government) refused to cooperate with her and withdrew its financial support of the NCWK. Without assistance from the government, the organization was left with few means of support. Over the next several years, the NCWK did its best to represent the women of Kenya. At the same time, the organization raised awareness of environmental concerns. Wangari won reelection as chairperson of the NCWK every year until she stepped down in 1987.

When elections for Kenya's Parliament were held in 1982, Wangari decided to run for the seat representing her home district of Nyeri. She had never considered running for office before, despite her connection to politics through her ex-husband. Over the years, however, many of her friends had encouraged her to run. One reason for Wangari's reluctance was the fact that not many women served in Kenya's Parliament at the time. Between 1980 and 1988, only two were elected. According to Kenyan law, running for office also meant that she would have to give up her job at the university. Though Wangari knew she would face fierce opposition, she thought the time had come to enter the political arena. Years later, she described in her autobiography what led her to make this momentous decision: "African women in general need to know that it's okay for them to be the way they are … and to be liberated from fear and from silence."

It was not long before Wangari learned just how deeply opposed the Kenyan government was to her

Through the National Council of Women of Kenya, Wangari raised awareness of environmental concerns by encouraging farmers and women to plant such native food crops as roots, yams, and cassava to ensure food for the household (as shown below).

candidacy. Shortly after resigning from the university, Wangari was informed by the committee charged with overseeing the election that she was not registered to vote. When Wangari disputed this claim, the committee explained that she should have reregistered in the 1979 elections. Because she failed to do so, she would not be able to run for office. Wangari was convinced that the government had created an excuse to keep her out of Parliament. Nevertheless, she was not about to give up without a fight. Accusing the committee of illegal action, Wangari took the Kenyan government to court. In the end, the judge appointed to the case ruled in favor of the committee. Wangari was declared ineligible to run for Parliament.

Once again, Wangari had lost in court, and justice had not been served. Returning to the university, she explained what had happened and asked to have her job back as the head of the Department of Veterinary Anatomy. However, the administration explained that her job had been given to someone else. Wangari was stunned. After 16 years of service, she had been replaced—and in less than a 12-hour period! The administration also explained that she was ineligible to receive any of the usual benefits, including her pension. The following day, as Wangari was on her way to court to contest the electoral committee's decision, officials from the university arrived at her home. They told her she would have to vacate the house immediately since only faculty members were permitted to live there. In less than three days, Wangari had lost her job and her home. The future had never looked so dark.

CHAPTER 3

Warrior for the Environment

The Green Belt Movement

Wangari was not about to admit defeat, however, despite losing her job and having to move her family to a smaller house. She put most of her energy into the NCWK. Though it was a poor organization and had limited resources, Wangari remained its chairperson and was determined to do what she could for the women of Kenya. She also began to develop an idea that had been with her for some time. At the celebration of World Environment Day in 1977, the NCWK had planted seven trees in Nairobi's Kamukunji Park. Those trees had been referred to at the time as a "green belt" that adorned the dry and barren land of Kenya. That moment had planted a seed in Wangari's mind, and it was about to bear fruit. The Green Belt Movement, which had started as a campaign of the NCWK, was about to take on a life of its own.

In August 1981, Wangari was presented with an opportunity that would change the course of her life. That month, Kenya hosted a United Nations conference on new and renewable—or "green"—sources of energy. This issue was becoming more and more important to the international community, and the NCWK's goals fit well into the conference's agenda. For two weeks, the delegates of the conference discussed a plan of action to promote green energy and good management of the world's forests. They also organized a march in Nairobi's Uhuru ("Freedom") Park to raise public awareness. During the conference, Wangari met many people from industrialized and developing countries who were interested in the

Green Belt Movement. At the same time, she wrote a proposal requesting money and support from the United Nations Voluntary Fund for the Decade of Women, which had been established at the 1975 Mexico City conference.

The following year, Wangari was busy working in her NCWK office when a man named Wilhelm Elsrud walked in. "I'm looking for Wangari Maathai," he announced. When Wangari identified herself, Elsrud explained that he was the executive director of the Norwegian Forestry Society. "We want to see if we can partner with you," he added. The two of them talked, and Wangari showed Elsrud some of the tree nurseries that she and her colleagues had planted. Elsrud was impressed with what he saw. He asked Wangari if she was interested in coordinating her

In 1977, Wangari founded the environmental organization the Green Belt Movement, which became the largest tree-planting project in Africa. The organization also focuses on environmental conservation and women's rights.

efforts with the Norwegian Forestry Society. Because Wangari was still looking for a full-time job and the position came with a small salary, she accepted. Shortly afterward, the request for funds she had made to the United Nations the year before was approved. The amount of the grant took Wangari by surprise—$122,700 U.S. dollars in total. It was more money than she had ever seen in her life.

The Green Belt Movement was now in full swing. The funds provided by the United Nations and the Norwegian Forestry Society allowed the organization to expand its activities. Their support also gave the move-

> *Planting trees was necessary and important work, but Wangari became convinced of the need to "plant" ideas as well.*

ment a measure of authority. As the size and scope of the Green Belt Movement grew, Wangari began to reconsider its mission. Planting trees was necessary and important work, but Wangari became convinced of the need to "plant" ideas as well. She began to organize "civic and environmental education" seminars in the communities where the Green Belt Movement was active. Wangari wanted the people of Kenya to understand why they did not have enough clean water, why the land was losing its topsoil, and why the infrastructure of the country was falling apart. She said the government had a hand in these problems, but she also emphasized that regular people, as citizens of Kenya, had a responsibility to do something about it. "It is your land," Wangari said. "You own it, but you are not taking care of it."

In July 1985, the third United Nations conference on women's issues was held in Nairobi. During the conference, Wangari explained what the Green Belt Movement was doing in Kenya. She also arranged for the visiting delegates to hear from women who lived in the rural parts of the country and how Wangari's organization had affected their lives. The following year, the movement expanded its work to other African countries that had serious environmental problems. Within three years, the Pan-African Green Belt Network was operating in 15 African nations, including Ethiopia, Tanzania, Uganda, Rwanda, and Mozambique.

While Wangari received numerous awards for her work, the Kenyan government remained opposed to

Kenyan community members tend to seedlings in a Green Belt Movement tree nursery. Eventually, the movement established more than 6,000 tree nurseries and grew to several hundred thousand members.

her. President Moi's regime had begun to fear the power and influence of Wangari's organization. In 1987, the government demanded that the Green Belt Movement separate itself from the NCWK. Without the support of the NCWK, Moi expected the Green Belt Movement to fall apart. Wangari was forced to resign as chairperson of the NCWK, but the Green Belt movement survived—and thrived. Eventually, the organization established more than 6,000 tree nurseries and counted among its members several hundred thousand men and women. By the early 2000's, the Green Belt Movement had planted more than 30 million trees in Kenya alone.

Struggles with the Government

In the late 1980's, the Kenyan government began to consolidate its power. In 1969, then-President Kenyatta had effectively put an end to Kenya's multiparty system. Since then, one political party, the Kenyan African National Union (KANU), had governed the country. Like many other African nations after achieving independence, Kenya became a dictatorship. Kenyatta emerged as a "strong man" president who did not allow opposition to his rule. While many people continued to disagree with Kenyatta and his policies, the most vocal ones were arrested by the government. When Daniel arap Moi became president in 1978 after Kenyatta's death, many people initially hoped that he would bring reform to Kenya. Moi released the 26 political prisoners that had been arrested during Kenyatta's presidency. However, any hopes for a return to democracy were soon crushed.

In June 1982, Parliament declared KANU's one-party rule to be official, and people who opposed the government were dealt with more and more harshly. People whom Moi's regime considered as a threat were harassed and intimidated. Some were arrested and tortured while in custody; others fled the country.

At first, the Kenyan government did not concern itself with the Green Belt Movement. It was perceived as just a few women planting trees here and there. When Moi's regime realized that Wangari's organization was teaching the people of Kenya to stand up for their rights, they began to take notice. As the Green Belt Movement spread and grew, so did opposition by the Kenyan government. It was troubled by the movement's activities and came up with various ways to stop the movement. One of the first steps the government took was to invoke an old law from the time when Kenya was still a colony of the United Kingdom. This law made it illegal for more than nine people to meet in one place without first obtaining permission from the government. Because most groups in the Green Belt Movement had between 15 and 30 members, this posed a problem. By this time, however, the movement had planted thousands of trees across the country. Many people in Kenya understood the value of this work and were not going to let the government prevent it.

In 1988, national elections were held in Kenya, and many people who supported greater political open-

> *As the Green Belt Movement spread and grew, so did opposition by the Kenyan government.*

ness used this opportunity to challenge the government. The Green Belt Movement took part as well. Despite the government's heavy-handed tactics, Wangari refused to let her organization's activities be limited. She and her colleagues joined other pro-democracy groups across Kenya and helped people register to vote. Unfortunately, the electoral process was plagued by corruption. President Moi's regime was determined to stay in power, no matter what it took. Those who supported Moi and his policies were declared winners across the board. After the elections, Kenya's Parliament passed a law limiting the power of the courts and the press. The *Daily Nation,* one of the country's most widely read newspapers, was banned for several months. Despite the fraud employed by the government to stay in power, Wangari and many others who had fought for the return of democracy refused to give up.

> *Wangari and many others who had fought for the return of democracy refused to give up.*

The following year, the Kenyan government announced its plans to build a 60-story building in Uhuru Park. The proposed building—the Kenya Times Media Trust Complex—was to become the new headquarters of KANU and house the *Kenya Times,* the ruling party's official newspaper. As part of the building project, a statue of President Moi was to be erected in the park as well. This news greatly distressed Wangari. Uhuru Park was one of the few natural environments in the sprawling metropolis of Nairobi where people could gather for recreation. She was convinced that construction of this skyscraper would fundamentally change the character of Uhuru Park and the role it played in the lives of Nairobi's citizens. She knew that something had to be done to stop the government's plans.

On Oct. 3, 1989, Wangari wrote to the managing director of the *Kenya Times*. In her letter, which contained the official logo of the Green Belt Movement at the top, Wangari urged him not to build in Uhuru Park. She also wrote a letter to President Moi himself. Receiving no response from the government, Wangari reached out to several influential people whom she thought would take her plea seriously. Among them was the director of the National Museums of Kenya. Wangari explained that the construction project in Uhuru Park would require the demolition of two of Nairobi's historic buildings, but he refused to support her. When the Kenyan government finally responded, it was not to Wangari directly. The minister for lands and housing told the *Daily Nation* that those who opposed the building project were "ill-informed." Members of Parliament, wishing to discredit Wangari, called the Green Belt Movement a "bogus organization" run by "a bunch of divorcées."

Despite Wangari's protests, the groundbreaking for the new complex in Uhuru Park took place on November 15. Unwilling to give up, Wangari sought an injunction from Kenya's High Court to halt construction. Her case was thrown out less than a month later. However, public debate over the building project was gaining strength. Many professional organizations, including the Architectural Association of

Kenya, were now siding with Wangari. Several newspapers from around the world also covered the story. Alerted by some of their environmentally aware citizens, foreign governments and investors began to raise questions about the need to build in Uhuru Park. In the end, the pressure that was mounting on President Moi's regime became too much. On Jan. 29, 1990, the government announced that it was drastically cutting back its plans to build in Uhuru Park. Wangari had won her battle, but she was certain there would be more to come.

Freedom Corner

The next years were full of challenges for Wangari. Though she had won a great victory against the Kenyan government, President Moi had his revenge against her. Late in 1989, the Green Belt Movement was evicted from its government-owned offices. With no other recourse, Wangari was forced to move the organization into her home. An audit (an examination of the organization's business accounts) by the government soon followed. The public attitude of President Moi's regime toward Wangari and her organization remained hostile. At the same time, Wangari realized she was now a political figure in Kenya and could not afford to stay silent. However, she was not alone in her ongoing struggle with the government. Many of the country's prominent politicians joined her in calling for a return to a multiparty system.

On July 7, 1990, a large pro-democracy rally was held in Kamukunji Park. Thirteen years earlier, Wangari and the NCWK had planted seven trees there,

marking the birth of the Green Belt Movement. The
following year, Jaramogi Oginga Odinga, the first
vice-president of Kenya, founded the Forum for the
Restoration of Democracy (FORD). Because of Wangari's high-profile struggle against the government in
Uhuru Park, she was now seen as an advocate for
human rights as well as the environment. For this
reason, Oginga Odinga invited her and many others
to join FORD as an opposition force to President
Moi's one-party rule. FORD
was soon declared illegal by the
government. However, it
planned another pro-democracy rally in Kamukunji Park in
November 1991. To stop the
rally from taking place, the
Nairobi police cordoned off the park grounds. Despite
the government's ban, hundreds of demonstrators
showed up. The police used tear gas and rubber bul-
lets to disperse the crowd. Several opposition leaders
and journalists were arrested, and at least two people
were killed. In the end, pressure for a multiparty
system proved too great. President Moi agreed to
schedule national elections at the end of 1992.

Wangari realized she was now a political figure in Kenya and could not afford to stay silent.

In January of that year, Wangari met with the
leaders of FORD to discuss how to take their pro-
democracy movement forward. During the meeting,
the group received a telephone call informing them
about a rumor concerning President Moi. According
to this rumor, the Kenyan army was planning a coup
to overthrow Moi. Immediately, Wangari and her
colleagues were suspicious. If Moi was looking for a

way to cancel the elections at the end of the year, a government-sponsored coup would be the perfect way to do so. Wangari and the others thought this rumor might have been started by the government itself to silence the opposition and hold on to power. The leaders of FORD were also told that some of them had been targeted for assassination. Upon learning that her name was on the list, Wangari was "chilled to the bone," but she refused to give in to fear.

Wasting no time, Wangari and the leaders of FORD informed the press. They thought that speaking out right away would keep them alive and protect other Kenyans who would likely be murdered if the rumors were true. Wangari and several of her colleagues made their way to Chester House in downtown Nairobi, where many foreign journalists had their offices. Once there, they issued a statement

Wangari's Green Belt Movement empowers Kenyan women to stand up for their rights. It also has mobilized communities, especially rural women, in Kenya, to protect the environment by planting millions of trees.

warning about the possibility of a coup. They also called for the date of the general election to be moved up. After making their statement, Wangari and the others scattered. When she reached her house, Wangari was told that several members of FORD's leadership had been arrested. In that instant, she decided to barricade herself in her home.

Before long, the Nairobi police arrived at the front gate of Wangari's residence, but she refused to let them in. "Open your door!" they called out. "I'm not opening it," Wangari replied. "I know you want to arrest me." With those words, a standoff began that lasted three days. Inside her besieged home, Wangari explained her case to as many Kenyan and international reporters as she could. Some she talked to on the telephone. Others dared to jump the fence around her house to speak with her in person. On the third day of the siege, the police lost their patience. Though some of the officers were sympathetic to the pro-democracy movement, they had a duty to perform. They broke down the door of Wangari's home and arrested her. She was pushed into a car and driven to a police station.

At the police station, Wangari was formally charged with spreading malicious rumors as well as treason against the Republic of Kenya. These were serious charges, and the charge of treason carried the death penalty. In prison again, Wangari found her second experience to be much more difficult. She was now 52 years old, had arthritis in both knees, and suffered from back pain. Alone in a cold, wet cell, Wangari was given little food and no blanket. By the time of her hearing, she was weak from hunger and in so much pain that she had to be carried into court by four strong policewomen. Fortunately, the judge in charge of Wangari's case treated her fairly. Like her codefendants, however, Wangari was required to pay a substantial bail and reappear in court on a regular basis. The government required these measures so that, by design, their work in the pro-democracy movement was made more difficult.

After her sentencing, Wangari was carried out of the courtroom. As she was put into an ambulance bound for Nairobi Hospital, she was overwhelmed by the large number of people who had gathered to show support for her and the pro-democracy movement. Among the crowd were members of the women's rights group Mothers in Action. The group held aloft a banner that said, "Wangari, brave daughter of Kenya, you will never walk alone again." These words warmed Wangari's heart. She was brought to tears when she saw how many people wished her well and understood what it took to fight for the future of her country. She soon realized that her supporters were not only within the borders of Kenya.

When Wangari was arrested, her colleagues in the Green Belt Movement had sent word that she was in danger. Friends of hers in such global organizations as the United Nations, the Hunger Project, and the Women's Environment and Development Organization, among others, all rallied to her cause. Several U.S. senators also made their voices heard. Among them were Al Gore, future vice president of the United States, and Edward Kennedy, the younger brother of the late U.S. president John F. Kennedy.

They cautioned President Moi's regime that arresting pro-democracy figures could damage relations between the United States and Kenya.

In February 1992, Wangari left Nairobi Hospital and continued her recuperation at home. Still using her house as an office, she resumed conducting the Green Belt Movement's business there. However, she was surprised to find out that many of her colleagues were afraid to meet with her there—or anywhere else, for that matter. They were convinced that Wangari remained a target of the Kenyan government. Nevertheless, members of the Release Political Prisoners campaign came by regularly to discuss how to promote democracy and human rights in Kenya. Meeting with a group of women whose sons were in prison, Wangari told them they should petition Kenya's attorney general for *amnesty*, that is, an official pardon from the government. Wangari also offered to provide them with moral support and serve as their translator with the attorney general because the women spoke only Kikuyu, which was not one of the country's official languages. They agreed to meet in Uhuru Park and walk together to the office of the attorney general from there.

On February 28, Wangari and a handful of other women met with the attorney general. The women explained their case, and the meeting seemed to go well. Afterward, Wangari announced that they were going to return to Uhuru Park and wait for the young

When Wangari was arrested, her colleagues in the Green Belt Movement had sent word that she was in danger.

men to be released. This surprised the attorney general. "Don't go to the park," he replied. "Go home. We've received your petition, and we'll review the cases." By this time, however, Wangari understood how the Kenyan government worked. Its officials never really listened and rarely did what they promised. Ignoring the attorney general's advice, she and the other women went to Uhuru Park and made camp at the intersection of Uhuru Highway and Kenyatta Avenue. There, they were joined by others, mostly men, who supported their cause and wanted to make sure they would be safe in the park during the night.

When evening arrived, Wangari and her supporters lit 52 candles—one for each of the young men being held as prisoners by the government. They came close to causing a traffic jam. People from all over Nairobi slowed down their cars as they drove by the park to see what was happening. Pedestrians came by as well to ask the women what they were doing. Wangari explained the situation and said they were on a hunger strike until the government released all its political prisoners. By the time the sun set, the gathering included more than 50 women, most of whom were mothers and relatives of Kenya's political prisoners. Many others joined them to show their support, donating money or providing water to drink. One man gave them a large tent to shelter them from the elements. To keep their spirits up, Wangari and the women sang hymns and songs about freedom.

By dawn the following day, the women had still not been reunited with their imprisoned sons. A second day passed with no change. The third day of

the hunger strike was a Sunday, and so Wangari suggested they hold a church service. As people in Nairobi left their own churches that day, many joined the service being held in Uhuru Park. The gathering that had started with Wangari and a handful of women was now a crowd of several hundred people. Wangari decided to put up a sign. She asked some of her friends to prepare a large board and bring it to the park. On it they wrote the words "Freedom Corner." That section of Uhuru Park has been known by that name ever since.

. . . she was more determined than ever to make a difference and fight for what she knew to be right.

During those three days, people came from all over Nairobi to tell their stories about how they had suffered at the hands of Kenya's government.

On March 3, the Nairobi police descended on Uhuru Park. Using tear gas and batons, they began to remove the peaceful protesters from Freedom Corner. In the chaos that followed, Wangari was struck on the head and knocked unconscious. She was taken to the hospital. When she was strong enough to speak, Wangari called a press conference. With a black eye and a baseball-sized lump on her head, she told reporters that police claims that she had incited a riot were false. Wangari added that neither she nor the other women would be silenced. "The mothers had a right to seek the freedom of their sons," she said. In response, President Moi called Wangari a "mad woman" who threatened "the security of citizens and the nation."

Throughout 1992, the nonviolent protest at Freedom Corner continued to attract attention in Kenya and other countries of the world. Wangari and her supporters moved their protest to All Saints Church, the Anglican cathedral in Nairobi, across the street from Uhuru Park. Their vigil ended in early 1993 when international pressure forced the Kenyan government to release all but one of the political prisoners they held in custody (the last one was eventually released in 1997). Upon hearing the news, Wangari, the other women, and their freed sons held a service of thanksgiving at All Saints Church. Wangari then returned home with an overwhelming feeling of satisfaction. By this time, the Kenyan government had also dropped all charges brought against her in 1992. This was one of the proudest moments of Wangari's life. Not only had she been found innocent of all wrongdoing, she had also helped to free 52 young men who had been imprisoned unjustly. She had also gained the world's attention in doing so. Wangari understood the struggle for the freedom of Kenya was far from over. However, she was more determined than ever to make a difference and fight for what she knew to be right.

Fighting for Justice and Democracy

Kenya's pro-democracy movement worked hard to make its voice heard in the 1992 national elections. Unfortunately, only a year after it had been founded, FORD fell apart as a political movement. Both Kenneth Matiba and Jaramogi Oginga Odinga claimed the leadership of FORD, and the party divided into two separate groups. Also, Mwai Kibaki, a former vice-president in the Moi regime, left the government and started Kenya's Democratic Party. Hoping to unite the opposition against President Moi, Wangari and many others formed the Middle Ground Group (MGG). Wangari was elected as the chairperson of the MGG, and she did her best to raise the awareness of the Kenyan people. During the campaign, she told them it was vitally important for them to go to the ballot box and reclaim democracy for themselves and their children.

They planted "trees of peace" in the valley in the name of the Green Belt Movement . . .

In June 1992, Wangari and some of her friends from the Freedom Corner protest formed the Movement for Free and Fair Elections. During the last six months before the national elections, they held town hall-style meetings, which were followed by open forums where all participants were invited to speak. Despite Wangari's tireless efforts, however, the political parties opposed to the Moi regime failed to rally around a single candidate for president. The elections were also plagued with corruption once again. Such tactics as voter intimidation and stuffing ballot boxes led to victory at the polls for President Moi and his supporters. Even so, the ruling KANU party won only 36 percent of the vote.

The following year, a wave of violence among Kenya's different ethnic groups swept the country. The conflict was most intense in the Rift Valley, where Wangari had lived as a child. Pointing to the violence, President Moi told the people of Kenya this was the result of a multiparty system. However, Wangari was convinced that the government was behind the "tribal clashes," as they were called.

In February 1993, Wangari traveled to the Rift Valley with a group of friends involved in opposition politics. They planted "trees of peace" in the valley in the name of the Green Belt Movement and called for the violence to end. Before long, the government demanded that they stop. President Moi gave a speech later that month in which he claimed Wangari had "masterminded" much of the ethnic violence taking place in Kenya. On February 25, one of her colleagues, Dr. Ngorongo Makanga, was abducted by a group of hooded men. Wangari became worried. When she received death threats, she began to fear for her life and went into hiding. Makanga recovered from injuries he received during his abduction. However, he was later charged with sedition by the Moi regime and sent to jail.

Wangari remained in hiding for two weeks. Moving from safe house to safe house, she was helped by church officials and foreign diplomats. The Norwegians were particularly involved in the efforts to keep Wangari safe. During this time, she was invited by Green Cross International, a worldwide environmental organization, to attend a meeting in Tokyo, Japan. The meeting had been arranged by Mikhail Gorbachev, the former leader of the Soviet Union. In a message to the Green Cross, Wangari explained her situation and said she would not be able to come. To the surprise of the Kenyan government, Gorbachev came to Wangari's aid and asked that she be allowed to travel freely. President Moi denied that any travel restrictions had been placed on Wangari, but his response to Gorbachev came too late for her to attend the Tokyo conference.

Eventually, the ethnic violence in Kenya died down, and Wangari was once again given the opportunity to travel abroad. Gorbachev's intervention on her behalf had raised her standing in the international community considerably. In April 1993, she was invited to Edinburgh, Scotland, where she received the Edinburgh Medal. The following month, she went to Chicago, in the U.S. state of Illinois, and received the Jane Addams International Women's Leadership Award.

In June, Wangari participated in the World Conference on Human Rights in Vienna, Austria. In 1995, she attended the United Nations fourth global conference on women's issues in Beijing, China. While in Beijing, she was reunited with old friends and associates from around the world. It was a moving and joyful experience for Wangari, to be with those who had supported her during her struggles with the Kenyan government. She was also happy to see that a generation of young women had grown up and joined the fight for the environment and human rights. Knowing that she and the people of Kenya were not alone in their struggle for freedom gave Wangari renewed hope for the future.

CHAPTER 4

The Politician

Election to Parliament

Kenya's national elections were scheduled to take place in December 1997. This time, the leaders of the country's pro-democracy movement were more determined than ever not to be defeated by the ruling KANU party. In September of that year, some of Wangari's friends and associates approached her about running for Parliament once again. However, this time they suggested she also run for president. (Kenyan law required that a candidate for the presidency be elected to Parliament first, but it was possible to run for both offices at the same time.) Wangari's friends argued that she should bring to mainstream politics what she had been doing with the Green Belt Movement for years. Wangari took these conversations to heart and weighed the pros and cons. With the opposition parties showing no signs of uniting around a single candidate, she decided to throw her hat in the ring.

On Nov. 20, 1997, Wangari announced that she was running for president as the candidate of Kenya's Liberal Party. The Liberal Party was one of 27 parties running in the elections that year, a huge increase from the 1992 elections, and Wangari was one of 15 people running for president. It proved to be a difficult campaign. Though friends and supporters worked hard to raise the necessary funds for Wangari, money remained an issue during the race. The press also challenged her more than she expected. Many journalists suggested Wangari could do more for Kenya if she stayed out of politics. Unfortunately, she did not get the chance she deserved to prove her candidacy at the polls. On the eve of the election, a rumor was spread that Wangari had dropped out of her race. The rumor also said that she had told her supporters to vote for other candidates. In the end, Wangari received only a handful of votes.

Wangari was deeply disappointed by the results of the 1997 elections, but she remained determined to fight for the people of Kenya. Her first step was to establish the Mazingira Green Party. (In Kiswahili, *mazingira* means "environment.") This party would allow future candidates to run on environmental issues like the ones championed by the Green Belt

Many journalists suggested Wangari could do more for Kenya if she stayed out of politics.

Movement. Before long, these efforts to protect Kenya's natural environment brought Wangari into conflict with President Moi yet again. In the summer of 1998, she learned that the government had plans to give large parts of Karura Forest, on the outskirts of Nairobi, to Moi's supporters. Wangari objected to the destruction of the forest. She wrote a series of letters to government officials and prominent journalists. With some of her colleagues in the Green Belt Movement, she then made her way to Karura Forest and began to plant trees.

Wangari and her supporters arrived at Karura Forest on October 17 to find a large section of it blocked off by a fence. A large sign declared the land to be "private property." A standoff between Wangari and government officials followed, and once again the eyes of the world were on Kenya. The standoff lasted nearly three months, and the fear of the government using violence to end it started to build. When Wangari arrived at the forest on the morning of Jan. 8, 1999, she was accompanied by six members of Parliament, several reporters and international observers, Green Belt colleagues, and supporters from other environmental organizations. They were confronted by 200 heavily armed guards. As Wangari and her supporters stepped toward the fence, one of the guards told them they could not enter the forest. "We're not trying to get into the forest," Wangari said, trying to remain calm. "We just want to plant a tree." The guard told them that was impossible because it was private land. "This is public land," Wangari declared, "and we're entitled to plant a tree on public land."

Taking a hoe in her hands, Wangari began to dig a hole. As she did so, the guards became aggressive, hurling obscenities at Wangari. "Who do you think you are, woman?" one of them shouted. A moment later, the guards attacked Wangari and her supporters. Many of them were injured, including Wangari herself, who took a strong blow to the head. With blood streaming down her face, Wangari fled the scene as her supporters scattered. Reaching her home, she called the police to inform them of the incident. The police, however, refused to arrest her assailants. Fortunately, one of Wangari's colleagues had filmed the attack. That evening, one of Nairobi's news stations showed the footage on television.

When it became clear the attack had been organized by the Nairobi police, it provoked outrage across Kenya and throughout the world. Kofi Annan, the secretary-general of the United Nations, defended

Wangari's actions and condemned the violence used against her. When groups of students in Nairobi denounced what the police had done, many of their protests were broken up by the government with similarly harsh measures. Nevertheless, student protests continued until Aug. 16, 1999, when President Moi announced that he was reversing his policies regarding Kenya's public lands. Shortly afterward, construction in Karura Forest came to a halt. Less than two years later, however, the government reversed course yet again and other public lands were handed over to Moi's supporters. Wangari immediately responded with a petition protesting the government's latest actions.

On March 7, 2001, Wangari traveled to Wang'uru, a village near Mount Kenya, to join some of her colleagues from the Green Belt Movement, who were

In 1999, Wangari, carrying a hoe over her shoulder, tried to enter Karura Forest in Nairobi during a Green Belt operation to plant trees. She and her supporters were attacked by armed security guards. Many were injured, including Wangari herself.

collecting signatures for her petition. While Wangari was in Wang'uru, she was arrested by the police and taken to jail without being charged with a crime. As word of her arrest began to spread, protests broke out across Kenya. Once again, the government's heavy-handed tactics against Wangari backfired, and she was released the following day. Continuing her fight for the environment and human rights, Wangari was certain the government would not arrest her again without cause. Unfortunately, she was wrong.

On July 7, Wangari took part in a rally in Uhuru Park. The gathering commemorated the 11th anniversary of the Saba Saba demonstration that had won free elections for the people of Kenya in 1990. During the rally, Wangari planted trees at Freedom Corner. Considering this to be a political statement on Wangari's part, the Kenyan government arrested her. However, they were forced to release her the following day. This was a difficult time for Wangari. She faced government harassment at every turn, and she was also dealing with feelings of grief and loss. Her beloved mother, Wanjiru, had died in 2000 at the age of 94. With her mother's death, Wangari was robbed of one of her greatest sources of support.

While visiting friends in the United States in late 2001, Wangari was given the opportunity to teach at Yale University in New Haven, Connecticut. The offer took her completely by surprise, but Wangari knew she could not turn it down. From January until June 2002, she served as the Dorothy McCluskey Visiting Fellow for Conservation at the School of Forestry and Environmental Studies. It was a wonderful opportunity for Wangari, and teaching students again after so many years did much to revive her spirit. Returning home in the summer of 2002, she felt ready to begin a new adventure. Kenya's national elections were six months away, and Wangari decided to make another attempt at winning a seat in Parliament.

After the failed campaigns of 1992 and 1997, Kenya's opposition parties finally came together to challenge the ruling KANU party. The new organization was called the National Rainbow Coalition (NARC). Wangari wasted no time in joining the organization because she knew she stood no chance of winning election without the support of NARC. The slogan of her new campaign was "Rise Up and Walk." This time, Wangari made quite a showing at the polls. On Dec. 27, 2002, she was elected to Parliament with 98 percent of the vote. NARC defeated the ruling

After two failed political campaigns, Wangari was elected to Kenya's Parliament on Dec. 27, 2002. Following her victory, Wangari is shown here taking an oath during the government's swearing-in ceremony on Jan. 6, 2003, in the capital Nairobi.

KANU party as well. After 24 years as Kenya's president, Daniel arap Moi was out of power. It was a joyous time for Wangari and others in the pro-democracy movement. They had helped to end a dictatorship, and they had done it without bloodshed. "We made a change in Kenya!" Wangari exclaimed. "We brought back democracy!"

The Nobel Peace Prize

On Dec. 30, 2002, Mwai Kibaki was sworn in as Kenya's third president. In January 2003, he appointed Wangari to the Ministry for Environment and Natural Resources. She would hold the post of assistant minister until November 2005. Though democracy had returned to Kenya and she had won a personal victory at the polls, Wangari knew that the hardest work lay ahead for her and the country. "Democracy does not solve problems," she later wrote. "It does not automatically combat poverty or stop deforestation. However, without it, the ability for people to solve problems … is, I believe, impossible."

On Oct. 8, 2004, Wangari left Nairobi to visit her parliamentary district of Tetu for a meeting. While she was traveling there in a government vehicle, her cell phone began to ring. Moving closer to the window to take the call, she was surprised to find that it was the Norwegian ambassador. He asked Wangari to keep the line open for a call from Oslo, Norway's capital city, but he would not say why. After a few minutes, the phone rang again. This time it was Ole Danbolt Mjøs, the chairman of the Norwegian Nobel Committee. "Is this Wangari Maathai?" he asked.

Identifying herself, Wangari brought the phone closer to her ear, wondering why he would be calling her. Mjøs told Wangari that she was being awarded the Nobel Peace Prize. It struck her like a thunderbolt. Turning to the other people in the car, Wangari broke the news to them as tears rolled down her cheeks. A moment later, they all had broad smiles on their faces. Wangari's colleagues embraced her and began to cheer.

Wangari was the first African woman and the first environmental activist to be awarded the Nobel Peace Prize.

The news spread quickly across Kenya and the rest of the world. Wangari was the first African woman and the first environmental activist to be awarded the Nobel Peace Prize. In its official announcement, the Norwegian Nobel Committee said, "Maathai stood up courageously against the former oppressive regime in Kenya. … She has served as inspiration for many in the fight for democratic rights and has especially encouraged women to better their situation."

By the time Wangari arrived at Nyeri's Outspan Hotel, a crowd of journalists was there to greet her. After a flurry of interviews, the hotel manager congratulated Wangari and made a surprising request: Would she plant a tree there? A member of the hotel staff quickly dug a hole as a crowd of onlookers and journalists gathered. Looking upon Mount Kenya in the distance, Wangari planted a Nandi flame tree and reflected on how appropriate it was to plant a tree in the shadow of that mountain. Mount Kenya had served as a source of inspiration for Wangari during her

childhood—and the countless generations that had come before her.

In December 2004, Wangari traveled to Oslo to receive the Nobel Peace Prize. During her acceptance speech, Wangari said how proud she was of other African women she had worked with who had played a large role in her accomplishments in Kenya. Wangari also spoke about how important trust and integrity were in the pursuit of justice. She expressed her hope that all the trees that had been planted by the Green Belt Movement would promote a culture of peace. Finally, Wangari called upon the leaders of the world to "expand democratic space and build fair and just societies that allow the creativity and energies of their citizens to flourish."

In 2005, Wangari addressed a commemorative symposium to mark the entry into force of the Kyoto Protocol in Kyoto, Japan. The Kyoto Protocol is an international agreement to limit global warming.

Controversy

Around the time that Wangari was awarded the Nobel Peace Prize, an unfavorable story about her began to spread across Kenya. It quickly captured the attention of the world's press. *The Standard*, one of the largest newspapers in Kenya, featured an article that profiled her career. The report claimed that Wangari supported a conspiracy theory about the origin of HIV/AIDS. Allegedly, she believed that Western scientists had created HIV/AIDS in a laboratory "to decimate the African population." Because of Wangari's scientific background, everyone who knew her thought this report lacked credibility. After she was awarded the Nobel Peace Prize, Wangari addressed the controversy. She denied having made such a statement or believing in the idea that HIV/AIDS had been created as a means of "biological warfare" by Western scientists or anyone else.

Privately, Wangari suspected that her political opponents were behind the article published by *The Standard*. It certainly would not have been the first time they spread rumors about Wangari to diminish her standing in Kenya. Despite this controversy and the lingering doubts it left in some people's minds, Wangari did her best to put the episode behind her. In the years that followed, she helped many Kenyan men and women living with HIV/AIDS. Wangari also raised the world's awareness of the devastating effects the disease had throughout Africa. "My hope," she said, "is that those who understand the virus better can work with those of us struggling to better understand and eliminate ignorance, fear, and a sense of helplessness. … We in Africa cannot win the battle against HIV/AIDS alone. … We need the critical encouragement, support, and cooperation from the rest of the world so that we win the battle."

Later Years

During the last years of her life, Wangari remained one of Kenya's most prominent political and social leaders. In 2004, she helped to establish the Economic, Social, and Cultural Council (ECOSOCC). ECOSOCC was formed to advise the African Union, a political and economic organization consisting of all 55 African nations, on many issues affecting the whole continent. On March 28, 2005, Wangari was elected the first president of ECOSOCC. She was also named as

Wangari and UN under-secretary Achim Steiner launched a $2 million tree-planting project to rehabilitate forests on Mount Kenya during a UN conference on climate change in Nairobi, Kenya, in 2006.

the "goodwill ambassador" of an ambitious project aimed at preserving the ecosystem of the Congo Basin in central Africa.

The year 2006 was a busy one for Wangari. On February 10, she was given the honor of taking part in the Winter Olympic Games. During the Opening Ceremony, which took place in Turin, Italy, she was one of eight flagbearers representing the Republic of Kenya. On May 21, Wangari delivered the commencement address at Connecticut College in the United States. The school bestowed upon her an honorary doctorate. Later in the year, the United Nations Environment Programme launched the "Billion Tree Campaign," and Wangari was instrumental in its implementation. The campaign was a response to the growing issue of global climate change and other challenges facing the environment. Wangari also

In 2006, Wangari (holding the bottom left corner of the flag) represented Kenya as one of eight notable women who carried the Olympic flag during the Opening Ceremony of the Winter Olympic Games in Turin, Italy.

received the Indira Gandhi Peace Prize in 2006. This prestigious honor, first given to Mikhail Gorbachev in 1986, is awarded by the Republic of India for outstanding contributions toward world peace and the advancement of freedom and human welfare.

In August 2006, U.S. Senator Barack Obama, who later became the first African American president of the United States, met with Wangari when he visited Kenya. Obama's father, who was born in Kenya, had been educated in the United States thanks to the Kennedy Airlift—the same program that enabled Wangari to study in the United States. Accompanied by Wangari, Senator Obama went to Uhuru Park, where the two of them planted a tree. During his speech to mark the occasion, Senator Obama spoke about the importance of freedom of the press in a functioning democracy. He called upon the leaders of Kenya—as well as its regular citizens—to safeguard this vital institution. "Freedom is like tending a garden," he declared. "It continually has to be nurtured and cultivated. The citizenry has to value it because it's one of those things that can slip away if we're not vigilant."

"Freedom is like tending a garden," [Obama] declared. "It continually has to be nurtured and cultivated."

Wangari joined forces with five other female recipients of the Nobel Peace Prize and cofounded the Nobel Women's Initiative. The organization supports women's groups around the world as they campaign for peace, justice, and equality. The other founding members of the initiative were Shirin Ebadi of Iran,

Mairead Corrigan Maguire of Northern Ireland, Rigoberta Menchú of Guatemala, Betty Williams of Northern Ireland, and Jody Williams of the United States. (Aung San Suu Kyi, the only other living female recipient of the Nobel Peace Prize, was under house arrest in Myanmar at the time, but she became an honorary member of the initiative upon her release in 2010.) Between Wangari and the other women, Europe, the Americas, the Middle East, and Africa were all represented in the initiative. Their first conference, which was held in 2007, focused on conflict, security, and women's rights in the Middle East.

Kenya's national elections were scheduled for the end of 2007. In preparation, President Kibaki announced the formation of a new political party that September. Calling it the Party of National Unity (PNU), he declared his intentions to run for a second term on its platform. During the primary elections, Wangari ran for a seat in Parliament as a candidate of the PNU as well, but she was defeated at the polls. She then joined one of Kenya's smaller political parties for the general election held on December 27, but she was also defeated in the general election. Many people—including Wangari—suspected fraud and called for a recount after the results of the election were announced. When President Kibaki was officially declared the winner of the election on December 30 with 46 percent of the vote, riots broke out across Kenya, resulting in the deaths of several hundred people. The violence did not come to an end until Parliament passed the National Accord and Reconciliation Act on Feb. 28, 2008. This act appointed Raila

U.S. Senator Barack Obama, whose father was born in Kenya, met with Wangari when he visited the country in 2006. The two planted a tree together at Uhuru Park in Nairobi. In 2008, Obama was elected president of the United States, the country's first African American chief executive.

Wangari appears at a news conference held by French President Nicolas Sarkozy (second from right) at the end of an environmental conference in Paris in 2007, along with European Commission President José Manuel Barroso (left) and former U.S. Vice President Al Gore, the 2007 Nobel Peace Prize winner.

Amolo Odinga of the Orange Democratic Movement party, Kibaki's main challenger in the presidential election, as Kenya's new prime minister.

Though she no longer held a post in the government, Wangari served the people of Kenya the best way she knew how for the rest of her life. She continued to plant trees across the country as the leader of the Green Belt Movement. At the same time, she helped to raise awareness of the need for environmental protection and defended human rights in Africa and around the world. Wangari also served on the board of the Association of European Parliamentarians with Africa (AWEPA). The organization was founded by European politicians in 1984 to help end apartheid (*ah PAHRT hayt* or *ah PAHRT hyt*) in South Africa. AWEPA collaborates with African countries to strengthen democracy and facilitate political dialogue between Europe and Africa. From 1948 until 1991, apartheid was the South African government's policy of rigid racial segregation.

In July 2010, Wangari was diagnosed with ovarian cancer. She faced this illness with the courage and dignity that she demonstrated again and again throughout her life. To Wangari, her diagnosis was simply another obstacle to overcome. Her battle with cancer lasted more than 14 months, during which time she was in and out of Nairobi Hospital. On Sept. 25, 2011, surrounded by her family and loved ones, Wangari Maathai died at the age of 71. The following day, her family issued a brief statement announcing her death. The news came as a shock to many of Wangari's associates because she had shared her diagnosis only with her family and closest friends.

> *To Wangari, her diagnosis was simply another obstacle to overcome.*

Wangari's death was mourned by people throughout Kenya, as well as politicians, human rights advocates, and environmental activists throughout the world. President Kibaki, Wangari's one-time rival, praised her "selfless service to the nation" of Kenya, and U.S. President Barack Obama celebrated her accomplishments. "Wangari's work," Obama later said, "stands as a testament to the power of a single person's idea that the simple act of planting a tree can be a profound statement of dignity and hope first in

Wangari attends the opening of The Global Seed Vault in 2008 in Longyearbyen, Norway, with Norwegian Prime Minister Jens Stoltenberg (right) and European Commission President José Manuel Barroso. The vault, near the North Pole, stores the world's crop seeds in case of disaster.

one village, then in one nation, and now across Africa." At Wangari's state funeral, thousands of tearful mourners lined Nairobi's streets to catch a final glimpse of her. Escorted by a platoon of Kenyan soldiers, her casket—draped in the black, red, and green colors of Kenya's national flag—was taken to Freedom Corner in Uhuru Park. There, in the place where she had challenged corruption, defended the environment, and fought for human rights, Wangari Maathai was laid to rest.

One Planet, One Humanity

Wangari Maathai's many achievements are perhaps felt most strongly in her native Kenya, but the long-lasting effects of her work have touched the entire world. One of Maathai's greatest legacies was her insistent call for the preservation and protection of the environment in which human beings make their home. "We all share one planet and are one humanity," she once said. "There is no escaping this reality." Though this message has yet to be embraced by the whole world, Maathai and her tireless efforts helped raise the awareness of millions of people across the globe. More important, Maathai's work continues today through the vibrant organization she left behind. Her daughter, Wanjira, has followed in her mother's footsteps, serving as the vice chair of the Green Belt Movement and project leader of the Wangari Maathai Institute for Peace and Environmental Studies at the University of Nairobi.

Wangari Maathai's life and career remain a lesson for the young people of today and tomorrow. Her work reminds us of the importance of believing in oneself and the virtue of never giving up. During her lifetime, Maathai faced nearly endless obstacles fight-

South African Archbishop and Nobel laureate Desmond Tutu (right) attends a memorial mass for Wangari Maathai in Nairobi, Kenya, on Oct. 14, 2011. Maathai died from cancer on September 25. She was mourned throughout the world.

Kenyans took part in the annual Wangari Maathai Memorial Walk in Nairobi, Kenya, on Sept. 25, 2015, the fourth anniversary of the Nobel laureate's death. The march is aimed at mobilizing African communities to raise their voices on climate change.

ing for what she believed to be right, and she was despised by those in power for daring to resist them. Since Maathai's death, however, many of the political opponents who fought her at every turn have come to celebrate her wisdom and foresight. The millions of trees planted in her name are now recognized worldwide as symbols of peace, hope, and transformation.

"No matter how dark the cloud," Maathai wrote, "there is always a thin, silver lining, and that is what we must look for. The silver lining will come, if not to us, then to the next generation or the generation after that. And maybe with that generation the lining will no longer be thin."

INDEX

O

Obama, Barack, 85-87, 89-90
Odinga, Jaramogi Odinga, 59, 67-68
Odinga, Raila Amolo, 87-88
oral tradition, 11
Oslo, Norway, 79, 81
Oswald, Lee Harvey, 24

P

Pan-African Green Belt Network, 53
Parliament (Kenya), 44, 56, 74; elections, 30, 37, 46-48, 72-73, 77-78, 87-88; Green Belt Movement and, 54-58
Party of National Unity (PNU), 87
Pittsburgh, Pennsylvania, 25
pro-democracy movement, 59-69, 72

R

racial discrimination, 22, 24, 31
Release Political Prisoners campaign, 63
renewable energy, 50. *See also* Green Belt Movement
Rift Valley, 14-16, 27, 64-65, 69
Roman Catholicism, 13, 20, 21, 23, 28; Wangari's conversion, 18-19, 26

S

St. Barbe Baker, Richard, 36
St. Cecilia's Intermediate Primary School, 18-20, 22
Sarkozy, Nicolas, 88

South Africa, 88-89
Standard, The, 82-83
Stoltenberg, Jens, 90
String, Maurice, 38-39

T

Tokyo, Japan, 69
tree planting, 34-41, 73-76, 80, 85, 88-90; Green Belt Movement, 51-54, 69, 88
Turin, Italy, 84
Tutu, Desmond, 91

U

Uhuru Park, 50, 66, 68, 76, 85, 90; protest, 63-67; skyscraper plan, 56-59
Unbowed (Maathai), 9, 47
United Kingdom, 8, 42; Kenya as colony of, 11-14, 20-21, 24, 42-43, 55
United Nations (UN), 22, 50, 62, 74-75; Development Programme, 46; Environment Programme (UNEP), 32-33, 38, 84; Green Belt Movement and, 52; green energy conference, 50-51; Habitat I, 39; Voluntary Fund for the Decade of Women, 51, 52; women's issues conferences, 33-34, 53, 70
United States, 27, 41-42, 63, 76, 84, 85; Wangari's studies in, 20-26
University of Giessen, 28
University of Nairobi, 25-28, 31, 41, 46, 48, 91
University of Pittsburgh, 25

V

Vancouver, British Columbia, 39

W

Wangari Maathai Institute for Peace and Environmental Studies, 91
Wangari Maathai Memorial Walk, 92
Wangeci, Agatha, 22
Wang'uru, Kenya, 75-76
Ward, Barbara, 39
Williams, Betty, 85-87
Williams, Jody, 85-87
Winter Olympic Games, 84
women's issues, 8, 18, 30-35, 46; election to Parliament, 47; status in Kenya, 14, 31, 42; UN conferences on, 33-34, 53, 70
World Environment Day, 39-40, 50

Y

Yale University, 76-77

FURTHER READING

The Green Belt Movement. http://www.greenbeltmovement.org/

Maathai, Wangari Muta. *Unbowed: A Memoir.* Knopf, 2006.

Nielsen, Larry A. *Nature's Allies: Eight Conservationists Who Changed Our World.* Island Pr., 2017.

ACKNOWLEDGMENTS

Cover: © Green Belt Movement

3 © Green Belt Movement

7 © Eliot Elisofon, The LIFE Picture Collection/Getty Images

9 © Pictorial Parade/Getty Images

11 © Hulton Archive/Getty Images

12 © Eliot Elisofon, The LIFE Picture Collection/Getty Images

17 © Priya Ramrakha, The LIFE Picture Collection/Getty Images

19 © Bettmann/Getty Images

23 © Green Belt Movement

24 © Harry Benson, Getty Images

29 © Green Belt Movement

31 © Bettmann/Getty Images

34 © Per-Anders Pettersson, Getty Images

36 © Green Belt Movement

43 © William Campbell, Sygma/Getty Images

47 © Green Belt Movement

49 © Micheline Pelletier, Getty Images

51 © Tony Karumba, AFP/Getty Images

53 © Green Belt Movement

60 © Wendy Stone, Getty Images

65 © Micheline Pelletier, Getty Images

71 © Green Belt Movement

75-77 © Simon Maina, Getty Images

79 © AFP/Getty Images

81 © Kazuhiro Nogi, Getty Images

83 © Simon Maina, Getty Images

84 © Clive Rose, Getty Images

86 © Green Belt Movement

88 © Jean-Luc Luyssen, Getty Images

90-91 © Daniel Sannum Lauten, Getty Images; © Simon Maina, Getty Images

92 © Green Belt Movement